HOW TO BECOME A
FEMME FATALE

CONTENTS

DEDICATION

To all my fierce dark feminine goddesses ready to release
their inner femme fatale.

WHAT IS A FEMME FATALE

Femme fatale is a modern popularized term that describes a particular type of woman. If you're reading this book, you are potentially interested in becoming a femme fatale.

Perhaps you've experienced feelings of being invisible or have had relationships where you feel powerless. Perhaps you've been cheated on in your past relationships or always find yourself being "the one before the one" for everyone you date. Maybe you're sick of being treated like a doormat. Perhaps you're sick of not getting the attention you feel like you deserve or tired of life not going your way.

In any case, you've picked up this book because you feel you're ready for a change in your life. You're ready to embrace your femininity and step into the real power that separates you from the rest. You're ready to learn the skills and habits that help you turn the tables and finally create the life you desire.

First, I'd like to congratulate you. You are now one step closer to embracing your inner dark feminine and becoming an unforgettable femme fatale.

ARE FEMME FATALES MANIPULATIVE?

The term "femme fatale" is French for "dangerous (or fatal) woman. In movies, femme fatales are usually secret agents, villains, and heartbreakers, painted as the bad guys of the story who allure their innocent victims into impending doom.

Many women become interested in becoming a femme fatale when they're in their worst wounded energy. That was my exact situation. I was hurt, deeply wounded, and sick of the life I was currently living. I was ready to revenge on anyone who had ever hurt me.

However, once I learned more about becoming a femme fatale, I realized that they are not always evil or manipulative. You can have manipulative femme fatales; however, being one doesn't mean that the essence of a femme fatale is manipulation. Therefore, in this book, I will not teach you to manipulate others or go out of your way pretending to be someone else to gain revenge.

Being a femme fatale means stepping out of your wounded energy into prioritizing yourself. A true femme fatale living for themselves does not see any need for petty revenge but instead lets karma do the dirty work for her. She might very well enjoy the sweet suffering karma unleashes upon her enemies, but she is too focused on her own life and her own goals to lift a finger to save them.

You might have picked up this book hoping to have a revenge glow up and make all your exes regret their existence. Trust me when I say they will, but not as you initially imagined. In fact, this is better. You will not have to waste a single bit of energy on petty manipulation, but instead, you will become a badass queen and the hero of your own story.

What a femme fatale is not

Contrary to popular belief, femme fatales are not the villains of the story. Being a femme fatale doesn't mean you must become a cold, bitter woman who wants to hurt people. You don't need to become an emotional manipulator scheming to stab everyone you know in the back.

A femme fatale is not a lone wolf who sits in her penthouse plotting the demise of her enemies. A femme fatale doesn't necessarily even have to have enemies.

Becoming a femme fatale also doesn't mean going out of your way to pour thousands of dollars to buy a new wardrobe unless that's what you feel like. To re-invent yourself, you don't need the latest fashion or the most expensive cosmetics. Better yet, you can become a femme fatale without any further financial investment. It's all about having a particular mental mindset and a way of expressing yourself.

Finally, being a femme fatale doesn't mean you need to change yourself to please others. You are not becoming a femme fatale because you must play a certain part to get someone's attention. One does not become a femme fatale for others; it is a journey you must take to serve yourself and yourself only.

Being a femme fatale can mean many things. Only you can decide what you do with the skills taught in this book. You can use your skills for good or bad, just like any other skill. Being a femme fatale doesn't mean you must become an angry woman pursuing revenge. You can use the process to heal, transform and improve yourself into the version of you that you've always wanted to become.

You can use the power of being a femme fatale to create the life you've always wanted. Sure, your exes will start to regret losing you in the process, but that is only one of the positive side-effects of embracing your inner femme fatale.

Good vs. bad

Along with the growing popularity of the "baddie" aesthetic, the concept of being a femme fatale has been popularized in modern-day social media like TikTok, YouTube, and Instagram. People have a general misconception about femme fatales, thinking they are "evil" or "negative" or that somehow being one means you are on a dark, vengeful journey ready to destroy anyone who crosses paths with you. In movies, a femme fatale is often portrayed as a woman who uses her feminine attributes, such as beauty, sex appeal, or other charms, to try to bring about the protagonist's destruction. Or suppose you come across a movie where the main character is a femme fatale. In that case, she is usually portrayed as having insurmountable suffering and guilt regarding her behavior and choices in life. Almost like leaving your femme fatale ways behind and finding the one true love to settle down with is the only thing that can save you.

Think about Natasha Romanoff in the Black Widow. She is an attractive woman that can seduce information out of anyone. Yet, she is deeply troubled by what she does, and falling in love seems to be her salvation.

It's like being a femme fatale is a burden that one can have, and you can only use it to bring about destruction. This is inherently wrong.

Becoming a femme fatale doesn't mean that you are becoming the anti-hero of your story. It means stepping into your power and taking advantage of your potential and the darker side of your feminine energy.

Becoming a femme fatale means you are ready to let go of being treated poorly, focus on your dreams, and be determined to get what you want in life. You're ready to start taking control of the direction of your life and ready to receive everything you ever hoped for.

The better way to describe a femme fatale is an untouchable woman. A woman that is content and confident with herself. A woman that draws other people to her because of her unique skills, talents, and characteristics. A woman that is confident with who she is and knows herself and the nature of others in a way that makes her unstoppable.

WHY SHOULD YOU BECOME A FEMME FATALE?

Two years ago, I felt like I was living my absolute worst nightmare. I felt like a complete loser, and unfortunate events kept reoccurring in my life. My life was not what I wanted, and I felt powerless to pursue my dreams. I constantly found flaws in myself and felt that there was concrete evidence that I was indefinitely a failure. Other people also seemed to pick up on this, not taking me seriously. The men I dated only played games with me, not considering me to be a woman they would fight to keep in their lives. I kept getting disrespected, ghosted, cheated on, and lied to by others.

I was in a dreadful job, where I was not only performing horribly, but my boss hated me. I did not connect with anyone from the office and felt completely isolated and a failure. I was in the worst shape of my life, exhausted if I was forced to climb a few stairs. Even carrying a grocery store bag felt like a struggle. My skin was constantly breaking out, and I didn't have the energy to put effort into my appearance.

I was operating from a wounded feminine energy that did not feel natural. Every day I felt drained and like I did not belong. I wasn't feeling good about myself or fulfilled professionally or personally.

I reached the peak a couple years ago when on my birthday, I found out my boyfriend of two years was cheating on me. Turns out, he was with the girl on my birthday instead of spending the day with me. I felt like everything in my life was going in the opposite direction I wanted to.

Hating your life and being treated wrong by others is not the worst problem one can have in life. My problems could have been worse. We all have different levels of obstacles in our lives. The problem is that we try to justify to ourselves that we do not deserve better. Just because we are lucky enough to be alive or have good health, we should be grateful for what we have and settle for a life where we do not feel happy just because our problems are smaller than what others have. However, the feeling of powerlessness as a result of everything negative happening in my life was something I'd never wish for anyone.

Once I discovered my dark femininity and became a femme fatale, everything in my life started changing. By learning the lessons I'm teaching you in this book, I gained more self-confidence. I reinvented myself and became a person I could finally feel proud of. Little by little, I started seeing changes in myself and in my surroundings. Not only did I change physically, my circumstances and the people around me changed. I now have a job that I'm obsessed with, friends that I love to pieces, a partner that adores me, and a pathetic, cheating ex-boyfriend who regularly floods my inbox full of sad cries wishing he was still with me.

Becoming a femme fatale is all about taking back the power that belongs to you. It means taking back the power in your relationships in a way that allows you to ensure you are being treated the way you deserve. Taking back the power in your friendships so that you have real, genuine friends who appreciate you for you, and avoid toxic and fake friends. Taking back your power in your life to make sure that everything you desire is effortlessly coming to you.

By intentionally reinventing yourself to the ideal version of yourself, the femme fatale, you can take back control of your life in a way that allows you to decide the direction you want your life to go.

Becoming a femme fatale will prevent other people from gaining control over you. It will allow you to see the true intentions of others and gain the upper hand over anyone who might want to hurt you. Instead of being a naive, innocent girl who gets pushed around in life, you are the main character who makes her own decisions and creates her own story.

By methods described in the following chapters, you will be able to put yourself first and prioritize your own well-being. You will be able to heal anything and let go of things that are weighing you down.

Getting what you want

Becoming a femme fatale ultimately helps you get what you want. A true femme fatale has worked through her limiting beliefs and believes genuinely that she can achieve whatever she wants. Practicing the skills of a femme fatale will not only raise your confidence but allow you to more effortlessly reach your goals.

When you step into your power, you will be able to reach your goals more efficiently, as well as other attributes. You'll be able to reinvent the way you look, the way you talk, and how you influence others.

Increasing your potential

Another reason you might want to become a femme fatale is that it will help you reach your full potential by emphasizing the characteristics you already have.

A femme fatale in movies written by men is overly sexualized and described from the point of fear towards female sexuality, almost to a point where the idea of being sensual and a sexual woman is intimidating, frowned upon, and something that will make others see you in a negative light. However, you must remember this is your story, and you can re-write how you choose to be seen as a femme fatale.

Femme fatales written and created by women are the heroes of their own stories. They are women who woke up one day, decided they deserve the life and the treatment from others they desire, and chose to start acting that way. A femme fatale created by women is empowered, someone who has stepped into her true self, finally ending the struggle of bargaining for her value. She has decided the time of negotiating between her feminine assets and the life she values is over and that she can have it all and have it her way.

And that woman can be you.

Becoming a femme fatale can help you prioritize yourself and put your goals first. It can help you have the cake and eat it too.

Revamp your love life

The habits taught in this book will be so powerful that you can seduce anyone you want once practiced with enough intent and consistency. You can get anyone to fall on your knees using specific seduction techniques. Carefully following the steps outlined can even lead to your ex trying to crawl back to you, like mine did.

The seduction techniques in this book are not manipulation techniques. They are habits and attributes that will make the real you irresistible in the eyes of yourself and others.

While you might deem it interesting to learn to manipulate your ex into falling back in love with you just to leave them hanging, that is not what a true femme fatale stands for. Trying to manipulate people comes from operating from a negative, masculine, wounded energy, which is some of the key elements you will first be guided to leave behind.

A true femme fatale has done the inner work to be able to function from a genuine and healed energy. Once you have started the guided inner work in this book, you will learn the healing methods of letting go of the anger you harbor towards the people that have hurt you and realize the true meaning of a femme fatale.

Narcissist vs. a femme fatale

A femme fatale puts herself as the number one priority in her life. She will not tolerate any lousy treatment and expects the best. She will let go of anything that does not support her values or aspirations.

Being a femme fatale is often confused with being a narcissist. However, there is a fine line of separation between both. A femme fatale prioritizes themselves and focuses on healing herself and her life for her own sake. She does not intend to be evil, even though her relentless brutality of prioritizing her own well-being sometimes might come across that way. Narcissism is defined as extreme self-involvement to the point of treating others poorly.

A femme fatale is glamorous and, above all, gracious in her behavior. She lives for herself and is guided by her values and morals. If she cuts ties with someone, it's because the person does not align with what she believes in. In contrast, narcissists generally see other people as pawns or puppets. Therefore, being a femme fatale does not equal to being a narcissist. However, it is possible that you can come across narcissistic femme fatales just like you can come across brunettes with blue eyes or brown eyes. The two are not intertwined.

GETTING STARTED: THE MOST IMPORTANT STEP

Now that you have a fair idea of what a femme fatale is, you're ready to start your journey. In this chapter, I will introduce you to the first and the most crucial step in how to become a femme fatale.

You've picked up this book because you've felt the calling to change yourself. Or rather improve yourself. You want to become a femme fatale. You're currently feeling that whatever you are, you still need to become something else you currently are not.

If you're reading this book, there is a chance that you've forgotten just how powerful you could be. How powerful you are.

Perhaps you've had some bad experiences that have made you feel powerless, not worthy, or that you're somehow less than others. Less than the ideal version of yourself could be. Perhaps you've tried and failed. You've been knocked into the ground, and somewhere along the way, you forgot to try to keep getting up. Or perhaps you have lacked the resources or the inspiration to pursue becoming the person you want to be.

It's time you started claiming back your power.

The first step into becoming a femme fatale is to believe you already are one.

That's right. Not after you've finished this book. Not after you've paid some influencer on Instagram 99 dollars for their online course or changed your entire appearance and the way you behave. Not after you've changed your wardrobe or managed to manipulate everyone in your life to believe you're some sort of an untouchable goddess.

The change begins with you.

The change begins with you first believing that you are already what you have always wanted to be. Before you can change what happens on the outside, you must first change what you think. And that begins by believing you already are the powerful femme fatale you wish to become.

You might think believing it in this part of the book is stupid. You don't seem like a femme fatale, and you sure don't feel like one.

That's the problem. To become a femme fatale, you must change how you think about yourself.

The essence of a femme fatale.

At her core, a femme fatale is a woman who is utterly confident with herself and happy with who she is. She shines brighter than everyone else because she embraces everything she is and uses it to her best abilities.

A femme fatale does not wish for her hair to be longer, her hips to be narrower, or her legs to be skinnier. She doesn't spend any precious time in the mornings in front of the mirror, looking at herself and hating every little detail about herself. More importantly, a femme fatale does not wallow in her mistakes and obsess about what she could have done differently in the past. She is who she is, and that is the beauty of it. A femme fatale is unapologetic, which is all part of the alluring charisma.

Think about how a person's confidence can affect their attractiveness.

We've all come across people that make us instantly realize they're insecure. In an instant, when the same person corrects their body language, they look more attractive. It's all in how you see yourself and how you present yourself.

You might think you're not ready to start believing you're a femme fatale. You think your looks are not there yet, or that your voice sounds like a confused parrot trying to fend off an enemy, or your clumsiness makes you afraid to go out in public. Think again.

When you're listening to an addict that wants to quit, they always say they'll do it tomorrow, the next week, or the following year. They're not ready to let go, and by saying they'll do something in a certain amount of time from now, they're only fooling themselves. Life happens now. Who you are, is who you are in this moment. There is no reason to keep delaying what you want to become.

Do it now.

Stop waiting.

How do I know you have everything you need to be a femme fatale? The first hint is that you're reading this book. You believed in yourself enough to begin researching the journey, so now commit to the rest.

Your beliefs shape your life

You might have already heard your life is what you think about. In fact, when you scroll through social media in today's world, it is difficult not to come across people who emphasize that your thoughts create your reality. It's easy to label it as something silly, but here's what it really means.

Believing you already are a femme fatale is the most essential first step in your journey. This is because you are who you believe you are. This is not some new-age hocus-pocus, but real-life facts.

Our beliefs influence our thinking, which in turn shapes our everyday behavior. This is difficult initially because the current contrast in what we believe and how we behave is vastly different. When you start to align your behavior, you will slowly begin to believe in yourself more.

When you try to convince yourself you already are a femme fatale, your brain finds the thought amusing and will try to resist the idea. This is because, in the beginning, your behavior contrasts with your thoughts. You are trying to convince yourself you are something, but act like something else. When your thoughts and behavior are in contrast, you will feel like you are lying to yourself, your brain trying to adjust your opinions or behavior. When you try to act like a femme fatale but deep down think you are not one, it will feel unnatural at first.

However, believing you are a femme fatale will slowly start to influence and guide your behavior. It will make you prioritize actions in favor of your thoughts, and slowly, you'll start acting more and more like the femme fatale you want to become.

Once the gap between what you think and do starts to narrow, it will begin to feel more natural. Only then will your decisions start to feel easier. The initial steps in believing you are something new will undoubtedly feel awkward in the beginning.

Not only do your beliefs shape the way you behave, but it also shapes the behavior of others. By adjusting how you think about yourself, you also adjust how others will treat you.

In a study made to prove the connection your thoughts have in shaping the behavior of others, men were observed making phone calls to women they'd never met before. In a control group, half of the men were told that the women they were about to call were attractive, whereas the other half were told nothing. As a result, the men who were told that the women they would call were attractive, were perceived to be more friendly and likable than the rest. Similar studies have been made in multiple contexts. The results have indicated that the beliefs one has before the interaction significantly shapes the outcome.

Believe that you are a femme fatale, and you are already halfway there.

THE DARK FEMININE ENERGY

Light feminine vs. dark feminine

You most likely have a rough idea of the difference between the light feminine and the dark feminine but cannot precisely pinpoint how they differ.

Feminine energy is generally seen as soft, caring, kind, and innocent. A traditional feminine woman is usually seen as a homemaker who wears polished floral dresses. She never goes against what her husband is saying. Light femininity is idolized and emphasized in society and media.

Recently I've come across quite a few feminine coaches for women over social media on Instagram, TikTok, YouTube, etc. It wasn't until I started to learn more about dark femininity that I realized most influencers in the femininity niche represent light femininity. Etiquette coaches, levelling-up courses, and housemaker channels focus on the sweet art of being a likable, well-behaved female.

Someone who is a light feminine woman is always agreeable and follows the rules. In the eyes of society, a light feminine woman is a saint and someone to look up to because she does not cause any harm by swimming against the current. She doesn't even speak up to herself because that would force her to step out of the light feminine.

If every woman was a light feminine woman, the world would be a very agreeable place to live in, full of arts, and crafts, baked pastries, and sweet kisses on the cheeks. The world would also be a very boring one.

Regardless of the societal praise light femininity has received, it is just one aspect of femininity. Like a yin to a yang, light and dark femininity are quite the opposites.

The foremost critical thing to understand is that society does not encourage women to embrace their dark femininity. But it's not for the reasons you'd imagine. Dark feminine women are people who stand up for themselves, do not play by the rules, and are not afraid of going after what they want. Society doesn't want us to work this way. It wants people to be agreeable, god-fearing obedient citizens, and femme fatales go against that ideal.

Whereas light feminine women are seen as angelic, traditional, and loving, dark feminine women are perceived as devilish, liberal, and known to use desire to their advantage.

The core values they believe in are the biggest separators of these two feminine energies. Deep down, both feminine archetypes possess similar qualities internally, but the dark feminine embraces all the dark sides of her personality, whereas the light feminine will try to suppress certain sides of them to gain approval from others. Dark feminine women tend to be more spontaneous, whereas traditional light feminine women prefer structure. Dark feminine women are usually seen as people who've had bad cards in life dealt to them, but that is mainly because they do not feel the need to suppress themselves to be approved by others. They do not feel like they need to hide different parts of themselves to be complete. Their own opinion of themselves is the only one that matters. They have done the inner work to accept themselves and, therefore, do not care about the opinion of others.

Feminine vs. masculine energy

A lot of people confuse the dark feminine with masculinity. The general assumption, usually due to popular movies, is that a femme fatale is all about action. She's a villain on a mission for destruction and revenge and will stop at nothing to achieve it. However, embracing your dark feminine energy has nothing to do with masculinity.

The masculine energy is all about action and doing. It's about owning, making things happen, following up, and controlling. Many masculine qualities are external, which means you can see these with your eyes. The way someone with masculine energy moves, talks and behaves. Someone with high masculine energy is focused on achieving and planning and is very driven and goal-oriented, almost to the point of tunnel vision.

In a nutshell, feminine energy is more about receiving, allowing, and being. Instead of direct action, feminine energy emphasizes attracting and manifesting. Making things happen with inner change, the outside changing as a reality. The attributes are more internal, qualities that a feminine woman develops in her inner world. A woman with high feminine energy is receptive, creative, and not afraid to show her vulnerable side.

We all have both feminine and masculine tendencies and habits but becoming a femme fatale does not mean you need to start embracing the man in you. Quite the opposite. Activating your dark feminine energy allows you to become feminine in a way that is alluring and irresistible to men.

Signs that your feminine energy is blocked

When our feminine energy is blocked, we might experience resistance and stress in our everyday lives. It might be hard to pinpoint where the friction is stemming from, but sometimes it might be an indication that your feminine energy is blocked.

1. Constant fear and worry

The first sign that your feminine energy is blocked is that you constantly live in fear and worry to a point where it's holding you back from doing the things and living the life you want.

You might be worried about money, constantly feeling like you need to make more and whether you'll be able to pay the next batch of bills. Perhaps you're constantly worrying about what others think of you, carefully trying to calculate your every move in a way that would give you more imaginary points in the eyes of others. Perhaps you're worried about aging, lack of time, or constantly stressed about work.

Living in a constant scarcity mindset is an alarming indication that your feminine energy is off balance. A true femme fatale does not worry about little things in everyday life. She does not let fear prevent her from doing something, nor does she sit at home, ruminating over things she can't control.

2. Lack of self-care

Self-care is a term thrown around in social media that revolves around having to buy thousands of beauty products, do Pilates workouts on a pink yoga mat and drink matcha lattes afterward. When we think about self-care, we often think it needs to include at least a facemask, bathtub, and skincare routine. Many people love announcing that a Thursday is their self-care day because that's when they do all the external groundwork for the weekend when they want to go out and look beautiful.

However, self-care is not just about nurturing your looks; it's about a lot more than that.

Self-care can be classified as improving and maintaining health, preventing disease, and combating any potential illness or disability. Self-care is not just sexy face-cream ads and pink bathrobes; it's about taking care of yourself physically and mentally in a way that will allow you to function optimally.

The lack of practicing self-care can even have consequences. When you don't feel great about yourself, the effects will often trickle down into other areas of your life and change how you behave and think. The lack of practicing self-care can even lead to adverse physical symptoms, unhealthy habits, mental difficulties, reduced performance in and outside of work, and decreased motivation to engage in social activities.

When your feminine energy is off balance, you'll often find yourself not taking the time to prioritize taking care of yourself. You're focused on surviving rather than thriving. When your feminine energy is out of balance, you often ignore your looks and health. It starts with small things like deciding to not shower in the morning before an important meeting. You think that others do not pay attention to the small details about you, so you choose not to either. Ignoring your split ends or dirty nails because no one will notice them anyway. Soon you find yourself letting go of your diet and taking on bad habits, thinking that a couple small slips will not make any difference. The negative feelings resulting from ignoring your self-care are easy to push aside at first but will ultimately make you feel crappy about yourself.

3. Hiding your real thoughts

The third sign that your feminine energy is blocked is that you find it difficult to express your genuine feelings and thoughts. You often don't speak up in a situation where you know you should and find it too intimidating to tell what is really happening inside your head.

When your feminine energy is unblocked, you will express your thoughts joyfully. Not only will you feel more confident in doing so, but you will also be able to do it in a way that others receive it well.

4. Seeking external validation

The fourth sign of blocked feminine energy is that you will prioritize the approval of others over how you feel about yourself or the things around you. When our feminine energy is blocked, we often have this quiet inner voice that's trying to tell us we're not enough. That something is missing. It's nothing but a slightly hollow feeling, but it will drive you to drive your self-value from being approved and praised by others.

A big part of femininity is to work on yourself and, as a part of that, heal your unconscious wounds that might drive any certain type of behavior that is not beneficial for you. Once you've unblocked your feminine energy, you'll have the ability to put more trust in yourself and not have to rely on the opinion of others.

8 WAYS TO ACCESS DARK FEMININE ENERGY

I: HEALING YOUR INNER CHILD

If you desire to become a femme fatale, you must not skip healing your inner child. Some call this shadow work or getting rid of your limiting beliefs. Our healing journey looks different for each of us, so call it what resonates best with you. Some of us have more work to do with healing our inner children, while others have more limiting beliefs or parts of themselves that they're trying to hide from others. All three concepts, however, are closely tied to each other and therefore discussed together in this chapter. If you haven't processed your shadow self, you most likely have many limiting beliefs you are unaware of. If you have many limiting beliefs, they can result from unhealed inner child wounds or unprocessed shadow parts of you. They are all interconnected, and to become a femme fatale, you must work on all three aspects.

Your "inner child" does not refer to a childish side of you or to any immature behavior. What people generally mean when they talk about healing your inner child are the subconscious experiences, behaviors, and thought patterns you've carried unconsciously with you for a very long time without you necessarily even realizing it. As long as you have not adequately processed the adverse events, thoughts, and emotions from your past, you are letting your past guide you and are not able to step into your full power.

A femme fatale is confident and comfortable with herself. She is not perfect, but she is happy with herself and does not get triggered by unprocessed emotions and traumas. One of the alluring qualities of a femme fatale is that she is so comfortable with herself in a way that separates her from the rest.

Acknowledge - First, you must acknowledge the parts of you that you need to heal to become a femme fatale. These can be anything from limiting beliefs to thinking that you are not good enough. You may have unresolved emotions or reoccurring worries that come from a more profound level or negative events in your life. Perhaps you've experienced trauma in your past and have worked hard to forget it and push down any emotions arising along with any memories related to the event.

Listen - Next step is listening to your emotions. Getting to the root of your problems might be difficult, and it might not be evident for you to understand where your limiting beliefs come from. By giving yourself a chance to be open about your feelings, you might uncover aspects of yourself you had not really paid attention to before.

Shadow work – By shining light on the areas of you that you do not usually pay attention to, you'll find out more about what's holding you back. It will help you to understand what parts of you still need healing.

Shadow work is often done by journaling. Here is some example shadow work prompts you can use to discover more about the unconscious parts of you:

General

How much do I rely on external validation? Whose
opinion matters to me the most?

Do I tend to resist or embrace change? Why?

What do I know now that I didn't know last year?

What am I insecure about? When did these insecurities
start? Who did I learn it from?

What was my favorite activity as a child? Do I still do it
today, and if not, why?

What are my parent's values, and how do they differ from mine?

What are some toxic habits I love? What pleasure do they bring me? Should I quit them?

What traits do I love in others? Do I possess those traits?

How do I react when something doesn't go my way?
Why?

What are some bad habits or behavior I want to change?

Why haven't I already changed them?

Honestly, am I happy with my life right now? Why/Why not?

Relationships / Intimacy

How did my first/last/most recent heartbreak change me?

Who has hurt me the most?

What is the worst way I've been rejected? Did it hurt me, and if so, why?

What are some of the patterns I keep repeating?

What is the most unattractive part of me? Why is it unattractive?

Who do I love the most?

Who have I loved the most but had to let go of?

What is my relationship with my parents like?

Is there anyone who could destroy you with just words?

What would the words be?

Take some time to reflect on these questions and ensure you're honest with yourself. Reflecting on some of these questions might feel like you're opening an old wound, which is what shadow work partially is. A wound that is not correctly cleansed might get infected or not heal correctly. Doing shadow work equals to you cleaning your wounds and making sure you allow them to heal correctly.

After a day or two, revisit what you've journaled and read them objectively. What do these things say about you? What can you learn from them?

2: MANIFESTATION AND VISUALIZATION

The second way to access your dark feminine energy is by learning to manifest and visualize. Manifestation is the process of using your thoughts, feelings, and beliefs to create your reality.

For those who do not believe in the power of the law of attraction, according to studies, there is a clear correlation between believing & visualizing you can do something and being able to do it.

An essential part of the dark feminine allure is having a mindset where you attract people, things, and circumstances in your life instead of relying on your masculine energy and hustling extra hard for everything you want.

By manifesting, you hold a clear image in your head of the things, experiences, people, events, or other attributes you'd like to manifest. A powerful dark feminine woman knows exactly what she wants and always seems to get it without anyone knowing why. The secret is manifesting.

The secret is to set a clear intention of what you want to attract and assume it is already here.

Let's do a fun exercise together. If you don't believe in manifesting, this is especially for you.

First, I want you to pick a color that, off the top of your head, you rarely see in your everyday life.

Now hold the thought of that color in your mind. Imagine different things in that color, imagine that color in different settings.

Next, go about your life as usual, and let me know how long it took for you to discover that color in your surroundings.

By focusing our thoughts on what we want and who we want to become, we slowly create our lives.

When you want to access your dark feminine energy, all you first must do is start to imagine what your life would be if you had unlimited access to that energy. Imagine everything you could do.

What would you look like? Sound like? How would you move? How would it feel to be you but with dark feminine energy? Feel that energy flowing inside of your body. Feel how it impacts everyone and anyone around you. How would others treat you? What kind of a life would you have? Imagine everything down to the last single detail.

Personally, I found this very difficult in the beginning. The key is to start very general and go deeper into detail as you advance.

If your attention seems to escape, set a five-minute timer during which you'll only focus on visualizing the dark feminine version of yourself.

3: PRACTISE MIND-STILLING

We've all heard about meditating, and while it's a perfectly good practice – mind-stilling is more effective for our situation. Mind-stilling is excellent for reducing anxiety, improving sleep, and enhancing your immune system, but most importantly for our purpose, it will allow you to access your dark feminine energy.

The dark feminine woman has an aura of cool, calm, collected energy. She is relaxed but mysterious. Her body language looks carefully planned out yet impeccably natural. She has quiet power, yet behind the veil lies a powerful creature. She is like a weapon that can be unleashed anytime, but she chooses to purr instead. She is filled with immense power, which she controls masterfully.

One of the critical difficulties of accessing your dark feminine energy is that you're stuck in your current state, which does not allow you to become the version of yourself that you need to access the dark feminine energy. Our inner worlds are filled with thoughts about everyday things, fears, wishes, hopes, and memories, all combining into a noise that prevents you from hearing the real you.

Mind-stilling will help you eliminate thoughts you no longer wish to have and help you channel dark feminine energy. It will also help you become more aware and able to focus your energy on yourself.

Imagine you have a dark, deadly power you must learn to control before it controls you. Imagine you're a superhero in a movie that's just discovered the first flickers of her power and now needs to learn how to regulate it. Mind-stilling does just that.

Practicing mind-stilling is very easy and straightforward.

First, sit somewhere comfortable where you know you will not be disturbed.

Close your eyes and take a breath in through your nose while counting to 6. Then release your breath through your mouth while also counting to six. Do this six times.

After that, while you still have your eyes closed, scan your surroundings for any sounds and noises. The way the wind is roaring in the background, how your computer is whirring. Maybe you hear little birds outside.

Once you've become aware of your surroundings, it's time to focus on yourself. Start becoming more aware of how your body feels. Mentally scan every inch of your body from head to toe. While doing that, think about the sensation in every part of your body and try to relax all of them as you go.

How does the top of your head feel like? How about your face, your neck, your shoulders? Do you feel anything you didn't realize was there before? Often, we realize we've been tensing a part of our bodies we did not realize we were tensing.

Once you're finished scanning your body, it's time to get to the core part of the exercise: stilling your mind. The purpose of this part is to not try to block your thoughts but to let them simply pass. The purpose is to separate you from your thoughts and help you realize you're not your thoughts. Imagine a powerful, large cliff on a beach. A cliff that's been there for hundreds of years, never altering, only slightly shaped by the waves crashing to it over the centuries. Imagine you're that cliff; the waves crashing on you are your thoughts.

Imagine how unwavering and strong you are. A cliff does not care about the waves; a cliff stands strong regardless. Imagine your thoughts appearing in your mind and then washing away just like waves against a cliff on a stormy night. Focus on this however long you feel comfortable.

Next, take a breath in through your nose while counting to nine. Let the breath out through your mouth while counting to nine as well. Do this practice nine times. Now do the practice with the waves and the cliff again. You might notice this time, your mind is much more still than before. If not, you might notice that you're not taking your thoughts as personally as you did before. You recognize that your thoughts as something that come to you, but you are not them.

Being able to still your mind in everyday situations will help you consciously steer your energy towards the dark feminine in situations where you want to unleash your full power.

4: DRESS FOR THE DESIRED FEELING

Dressing for the desired feeling is an important aspect of accessing your dark feminine energy. This means that whatever you want to feel, you should dress accordingly. If you want to feel powerful, you should wear something that makes you feel powerful even if there is no one else around. If you want to feel like a seductress, define what that means to you and how to dress for it. If you want to feel like a mystery, brainstorm ideas on how a mysterious woman would dress.

If you're unsure what you want to "feel", think about your overall goals. If your goal is to become successful in your career, your goal could be to feel intelligent, talented, and capable. If your goal is to attract a partner, you probably want to feel high-value and attractive. If your goal is to get revenge on your hateful ex-boyfriend who cheated on you, you probably want to feel like a prize who can make a grown man cry.

Imagine the dark feminine version of yourself that succeeds in pursuing these goals. How does it feel? What does she look like?

Dressing for the dark feminine energy is not only crucial in public when you're faced with other people but also in private. That's because the dark feminine energy is a feeling which starts with you. It's a form of energy that is only activated if you're truly living it. When you're at home, make sure to keep dressing for the desired feeling. If you want to become the most powerful seductress in your social circle, you shouldn't climb into ugly, unfitting PJs when you get home. Only wear pieces that make you feel special and aligned with your desired, dark feminine energy.

Dressing for the feeling you want to feel doesn't mean that you need to go all out and purchase a new wardrobe. Go through your existing ones, filter out the ones that make you feel the best, or figure out new ways to wear your old clothes. Dark feminine energy is about optimizing what you have and who you currently are instead of trying to become someone else by purchasing a costume wardrobe that doesn't feel like yourself.

Start with at least one piece in your current wardrobe that makes you feel like a dark feminine woman. What is it about this item that makes you feel that way? This will help you create a foundation for the future and help you replicate that feeling in other outfits or items.

5: GET COMFORTABLE WITH YOUR SEXUALITY

An important part of the dark feminine allure is to be comfortable with your sexuality. This does not mean that you need to make yourself sexually available to more people, but rather that you are more confident with yourself in a more sensual way and open towards your sexuality.

Typical light feminine traditional values revolve around innocence and coming across as someone who does not suggest intimacy or illicit thoughts about sexuality. However, a dark feminine woman embraces these qualities about herself and does not try to oppress them. A dark feminine woman oozes sensuality, and a part of that is being comfortable with your sexuality. Sexuality is a part of us, and it's time to accept it as a natural part of you, just like any other attribute in your appearance or personality.

Getting comfortable with your sexuality helps you access your dark feminine energy and embrace the parts of you that society tries to deem as "shameful". You do not need to hide certain details about yourself.

Embracing every inch of you makes you more complete in ways that the light feminine could only dream of.

Get familiar with your body

The first part of getting comfortable with your sexuality is becoming more familiar with your physical body.

Notice how I'm using the word "familiar" rather than confident. That's because to be able to accept and love your body, you must first know precisely what your body looks like. You must learn to look at it and accept it without shame. Many of us are stuck hating a certain aspect of ourselves and try to avoid seeing that part in the mirror. The first step towards acceptance is fully recognizing the current reality.

Try looking at yourself in the mirror naked. What do you see, smell, and hear? What does your body feel like? This might be very difficult at first because we are so used to feeling ashamed of our nudity and our bodies in general. You might feel the urge to look away and forget about the whole practice. Stick through it.

In the beginning, commit to looking at yourself in the mirror for 5 minutes daily. You can even set a timer.

Scan your body from head to toe, front to back. Is there something you haven't noticed before?

Your head might be flooded with negative thoughts about your body. Try and ignore them. This is the only body you'll ever have, and today you are the youngest you'll ever be. Make a conscious effort to focus on the things you enjoy about your body. Give yourself small compliments, no matter how forced it feels in the beginning.

After a while, you'll notice the voice in your head starts to become more kind. Your thoughts about your body will slowly begin to change. You'll be able to recall what your body looks like more easily and start to appreciate it more.

Explore what interests you

To become more comfortable with your sexuality, you must discover what you're really into. A dark feminine woman knows without hesitation what she loves to receive both in and out of bed. A femme fatale is not afraid to take the lead in the bedroom because she knows what she wants.

Do you know what turns you on? Or what turns you off? How have those things shifted over time? Keep a list of the things that you like and what you would like to try. In the same way, as you would keep a note of all the hobbies you would like to try, you can create a sexual to-do list that you refer to every now and then.

Dedicate an evening or two just to find out your preferences. Research literature, online sources, or videos. Block out your calendar, turn off notifications, and set your space up for the mood. Lighten up the mood and make it a fun and a positive experience for yourself.

Set a goal to find out your 3 biggest turn-ons, and do not stop before you've found them.

Don't compare yourself

It's easy to compare yourself to others and feel like you're not good enough. The problem with comparing ourselves is that we only see what others want us to see. In the world of photoshop and carefully curated Instagram feeds, we rarely see the truth behind what people post online. When we see ourselves naked, we might compare ourselves to others on the internet, but in many cases, the people we are comparing ourselves against do not even look like their photos.

Try to avoid comparison at all costs. A dark feminine woman knows she is one of a kind and therefore does not wish to be like anyone else.

Set boundaries and enforce them

A powerful dark feminine woman cannot be manipulated and hoaxed into doing something she does not want to do. She never ends up in situations where she feels uncomfortable because a dark feminine woman knows her personal boundaries when it comes to intimacy and does not accept anyone who tries to push through them.

You are the only person who can decide what you will and won't tolerate. You are the only person who can define what you like and what you do not like. You should never let anyone try to convince you otherwise.

A dark feminine woman never gives in on her boundaries to please someone else. She will never say yes to begging or convincing unless it's for something she truly enjoys. Making bargains with your boundaries exposes you to manipulation and risks you being played by men.

Make a vow to yourself here and now that you will never compromise your values and boundaries for anyone. You make the calls regarding what you want to do and what happens to your body. Anyone who thinks otherwise can be cut off.

6: FOLLOW YOUR INTUITION

One of the key elements that make the dark feminine seem like they have superpowers is the fact that they rely strongly on their intuition.

The intuition of a dark feminine woman is unlike no other. She can use it to her advantage to gain superhuman powers and enhance her femininity. Dark feminine women do not engage in activity that does not feel good for them, and they are quickly able to listen to their intuition to differentiate what is for them and what is not.

By learning to listen to your intuition, you will get to know yourself better in a more genuine and authentic way.

The first step in practicing your intuition is to practice quieting your inner monkey mind and start listening to your intuition. It might be challenging to recognize if you haven't practiced listening to your intuition before. The difference between your intuition and your other inner chatter is usually the easiest separated from the emotional charge of the inner voice.

Intuition is a very subtle thought that comes into your mind at any moment. Intuition is feeling or an insight about what you're currently experiencing rather than something that will happen in the future.

Your intuition can tell you whether something you're currently doing is good or bad for you, but it can't tell you anything about the future. Those thoughts are usually called anticipatory thoughts and are often related to anxiety, fear, or hopefulness.

Your intuition is also not an emotionally charged thought. Unlike anxiety and fear, intuition is such a subtle voice that you'll easily miss it if you don't pay close attention to it. Intuition is more like a feeling in your gut rather than a thought.

Once you've learned to differentiate the sound of anxiety and fear from your intuition, it's time to start practicing listening to your intuition.

Start small at first. You can use your intuition in the beginning in very small things, such as selecting items in a grocery store or selecting your route when you have a walk. Listen to the small voice of intuition. Do you recognize it? What does it say?

By starting small and advancing into bigger things, you will slowly learn to listen to your intuition better daily. Like any other skill, listening to your intuition requires daily practice; the more you do it, the better you become at it.

7: EMBRACE CHAOS

Life is constantly changing and never the same. Dark feminine women accept this and seem to master the art of chaos. They do not halter at the sight of change but embrace it to the point where they grow stronger each time. Just like a diamond is created under pressure, the dark feminine women are only made stronger as they learn to master the challenges of ever-changing life situations.

The first step to embracing chaos is accepting that you cannot control all aspects of life. The life you lived 10 years ago might have looked very different from now. Whether you wanted it or not, the life you're living now will most likely look completely different in another 5-10 years. The chaos of change is a part of life as much as the sun, the moon, and the very air we breathe.

Often when we experience fear of change, we tend to try to master controlling the little things and cling on to the idea that controlling them will bring us safety. We compensate by asserting extreme control over small things that make very little difference to the bigger picture in our lives. We try to control our habits, what we eat, and what other people think of us. We believe that if everything in our house or our jobs is under control, we are somehow safe from chaos.

The dark feminine women are not afraid of change. They do not try to cling to a sense of control but have accepted that everything has its time to die and be reborn again. The dark feminine women embrace life and the temporary pleasures because they are aware they are just that, temporary.

Under the surface, the need to control change in your life is a fear-based emotion that will only hold you in one place in life. A dark feminine woman is constantly improving herself. She understands that life has an unexplained, mysterious way of making your dreams come true.

We cannot connect the dots until the end of the story, so while the train is still moving, we might as well enjoy the ride.

A dark feminine woman is a powerful being who will successfully defeat every challenge life throws at her. If you think you're not powerful, let me remind you that you have survived 100% of your worst days.

Your success rate is 100%, and yet you still hold fear in your mind.

8: ACTIVATE YOUR CREATIVITY

Finally, the last way to channel your dark feminine energy is to do things that are creative. The purpose of this is to get you into a creative flow, which is a type of energy that allows you to get to the same frequency with your dark feminine energy when done correctly. Doing something creative is a great way to tune yourself into the feminine frequency.

To channel your creative, dark feminine energy, you do not need to be artistic, have any specific skills, or even be particularly good at anything. All you need is an open mind and the willingness to get out of your comfort zone.

When you hear people talking about creative endeavors, you often think about painting, drawing, or even sowing. These are very inside-the-box types of creative hobbies. Channeling your dark feminine creative energy doesn't mean you need to be able to draw or paint; it's about doing an activity that gives you the desired feeling.

For example, you could try dancing. Moving your body in a creative way that makes you feel seductive and feminine. Perhaps you can take up sculpture-making, creating sensual pieces of art as a token of your dark femininity. If you paint, conjure images and scenes that represent the energy you desire to feel. Beautifying your surroundings in a dark feminine way can also be a creative hobby that allows you to access your desired energy. Anything that gets you in the flow makes you feel like the dark feminine goddess you are.

HOW TO LOOK LIKE A FEMME FATALE

According to the general definition, a dark feminine femme fatale is the kind of woman every man wants to be with but knows they shouldn't. She is a temptation, a mystery to solve, and alluring in a way that is impossible to resist.

They stand out from the crowd with their appearance and are difficult to forget. In popular media, dark feminine women typically dress in dark or red evening gowns, skirts, and suits accessorized with furs, pearls, and high heels. While this is a very marginalized stereotype, you can follow certain tricks and tips to bring out your inner femme fatale.

Personal grooming

A femme fatale is someone who always looks put together. Investing in your personal grooming is the most important step in looking a little extra every day.

The first and the most important thing is practicing adequate personal hygiene. This might sound obvious to some but not all. Sometimes you might be neglecting your hygiene without realizing it. We've all been in situations where we're debating whether to shower in the morning because we're busy, tired, or don't really feel dirty. Always pay attention to your general hygiene if you want to become a true femme fatale. Pay attention to every part of your cleanliness to ensure you have nothing to hide and feel confident in every inch of your body. This is not only to make you look better, but you'll also feel better about yourself, affecting how you act and how others perceive you. When you're on a mission to take over the world, it is imperative that you feel invincible. Sometimes it can be just as simple as knowing that you do not have smelly armpits.

If you do not believe me, imagine the following scenario: you've neglected your hygiene for a few days and decide to casually pop into the grocery store. You notice that a hot guy is standing in the next aisle. Knowing that you smell like a bankrupt fish shop, what are the odds that you go and talk to the hot guy? The chances are that you keep walking, cursing at the fact that you wore your sweaty pants.

In contrast, imagine you feel great. You smell great, and know you look great. Your confidence to go talk to the guy is higher. This can apply to similar situations with acquaintances or any other opportunities. The point is not how you look but how your physical appearance makes you feel. If you feel the most confident in hair that is starting to form dreadlocks from greasiness and a birdnest, then by all means, embrace it, but for many of us, that is not the reality. We feel great when we feel clean and polished.

Your hair should always be clean and looked after. Your hair is the crown of your head and should never be neglected. Nothing makes a person look less put together than greasy, unbrushed hair. You might wear the most flattering outfit or makeup, but if your hair looks like old noodles, your overall image will suffer.

Invest in a good quality shampoo and conditioner because you're worth it. If you don't believe you are worthy of a good quality shampoo, how can you convince yourself to be worthy of anything else?

If you are on a strict budget, research home remedies to help your hair heal and grow, such as different oils and rice water. Home remedies are easier on your wallet, but making the extra effort to take care of your locks will benefit you in the long run.

Make sure to invest time in carefully selecting the correct type of makeup for yourself. Investing time rather than money into your cosmetic products is more beneficial because expensive does not equal good results in cosmetics. It is possible to buy the most expensive products, but if they're not suitable for your skin type, you're essentially wasting money. Spending time to investigate the ingredients and functions of cosmetic products and finding out what works best for your skin type will make you look better than anything else.

A femme fatale is someone whose appearance is well-considered and very well-put together. Pay attention to small details in your appearance and think about all the small ways you could enhance your looks.

Dressing like a femme fatale

The typical femme fatale we see in movies dresses in very formal clothing, but this is not very practical. If you desire to look like a femme fatale, the key is to dress for the occasion you're currently in. If you're going on a casual coffee date, don't wear a maxi-length evening gown. If you're in the office, wear something appropriate for the professional environment. The key is to wear occasion-appropriate outfits but with a flare. Play around with colors, accessories, and ways you mix different pieces of clothing to create an unexpected outcome.

A typical femme fatale prefers darker colors in her clothing over light tones. Think of dark green over pastel green and maroon rather than pink. Some of the typical signature style pieces of femme fatales include plaid prints, lace, satin, and sheer mesh fabric. Mix these to create your own unique signature femme fatale style.

More importantly than dressing in flashy evening gowns and revealing clothes, a femme fatale dresses in a way that suits her body type. Femme fatales are rebellious, mysterious creatures and none of whom are alike.

Find out your body type and how to dress to flatter it. Not everyone can wear a mini skirt or a bodycon dress, and not everyone has to. Being a femme fatale is all about emphasizing your unique features rather than trying to fit into a certain box.

The same applies to choosing the colors you wear. Red is typically seen as a seductive siren color. Traditionally femme fatales are seen as wearing black or different shades of red, but you should wear whatever compliments your features the most. Invest time defining what color palette works best with your skin tone and incorporate them into your everyday outfits where possible. Invest in a color analysis or use some of the free apps online or in mobile app stores.

In addition, learn about color psychology and how different colors affect people. This way, you can adjust the color of your clothes according to your intentions. For example, blue evokes feelings of trust, whereas yellow is associated with creativity and bubbly energy. By knowing the associated effects of different colors, you'll be better able to intentionally achieve your goals, starting from what you wear.

Finally, a femme fatale dresses in a way that makes her feel confident. Even though femme fatales are generally seen to dress very attractively or provocatively, they do not wear something just because someone else might like it. They do not wear tight clothes that limit their moves or revealing necklines just so that someone would notice them. They wear what they want to wear because it makes them feel like the dark feminine goddess they are.

Femme fatales will also wear whatever they want instead of being afraid of what others might think. Many of us have those outfits or items lying around in our closets that we bought because we loved them but have since been too afraid to wear them as others might judge us.

Have a look at your closet, remind yourself of what these items are for you and commit yourself to wear them all one by one until you're comfortable with the idea of wearing what you want despite the fear of being judged.

The closet of a femme fatale

A femme fatale has a closet where every item has a purpose and, more importantly, value. Every item exists because they add something to her general image and improve her appearance.

Before I became a femme fatale, my closet consisted of a big proportion of comfortable clothes. These are items that I would wear on daily bases, generally at home. They made me feel comfy but not at all like the person I wanted to be. If I wore these items outside my house, I generally felt frumpy, unattractive, and not really put together. These clothes were typically my worn-out sweatpants, baggy t-shirts, and stretchy jumpers, which had definitely seen their best days.

While these clothes made me feel comfortable, they did not support the image of the person I wanted to become.

Even if you wear these items in the comfort of your home without anyone else seeing them, they will still affect your image. Even when no one else is watching, you know what you're wearing. You know how you're feeling wearing these things, which affects how you see yourself.

How you feel about yourself when no one else is watching is vital to becoming a femme fatale. You should eliminate any clothes that make you feel like the opposite of a dark feminine goddess. Even when you go to bed, you should wear something that makes you feel like the alluring, sensual woman you are. A femme fatale does not go to bed wearing frumpy old t-shirts and long johns.

Objectively clean your closet and get rid of anything you don't see the ideal version of yourself wearing. If this is your entire closet, do the clean-out gradually by getting first rid of the worst ones while slowly replacing them with your dream clothes over time.

If you're open to acquiring new pieces of clothing, invest in statement pieces that can be used to spice up multiple outfits on versatile occasions. These can be anything from feminine accessories to scarves, belts, bags, or dresses.

Acquiring timeless pieces is the key to a long-lasting, high-quality femme fatale wardrobe. Imagine what you could see yourself wearing in 2-4 years.

Try to avoid buying trendy items in the effort of trying to look seductive or sexy, as trends usually do not last that long and tend to be very saturated. If you keep constantly buying trendy items, you'll end up looking cheap in the long run.

Regardless of the type of clothes you choose to wear, the clothes of a femme fatale are always clean, ironed, and free of dust, hair, etc. You should never wear pieces of clothes that are wrinkly or smelly. Don't double-wear your socks, and make sure everything always smells fresh. As a dark feminine woman, realize you deserve only the best.

HOW TO ACT LIKE A FEMME FATALE

Confidence

A femme fatale is confident in her skin and knows that there is no one like her. To tell the truth, we are all unique, and there is no other one just like us. The superpower of a femme fatale is that she leans into this quality and embraces it in a way that she is not scared to stand out of the crowd and is proud of who she is.

Femme fatales are never outwardly anxious and fearful as they have done the inner work to master their shadow selves and have become the masters of their inner minds.

Voice

If you've never paid attention to the sound of your everyday voice, now is the time to do it.

Femme fatales generally tend to speak in a lower tone compared to others. Not in a manly lower tone, but rather than a lower version of their own voices. According to studies, people with lower voices are perceived to possess more authority. In contrast, people with high, squeaky voices are seen to have less authority.

Femme fatales also tend to speak slightly slower than average women. This will make you seem like your words hold more power and really allow the listener to be hypnotized by your words. Femme fatales also take purposeful pauses between important sentences, making them seem more confident and knowledgeable.

Movement

Femme fatales move in a distinct way that is different compared to other women. Instead of being clumsy or quick with their movements, femme fatales almost look like they are in a slow-motion film. Their movements are smooth and slow and look carefully considered. This is because, in the initial stages of becoming a dark feminine, you must pay attention to how you move and practice moving in a more subtle, slow, and soft way. In time after careful practice, it will become your new normal.

Think about typing on a keyboard. Do your fingers just punch the letters while your body stays stiff? Or do your fingers dance around the keyboard in a movement that can hypnotize kingdoms?

Do you just grab a water bottle with a swift husk, or do you capture it with an embrace that makes anyone wish you were grabbing them instead?

Practice different ways of movement and find the best signature moves for you.

Walking into a room

One of the most crucial signature moves of a femme fatale is walking into a room in a way that looks like she owns it and everyone in it. This is not accidental. The good news is that it can be easily practiced.

When you walk into any room with people, take a long step to the doorway, and pause for just a few seconds. While you're paused, slowly allow your gaze to wander from one side of the room to the other. While doing this, slowly scan the people in the room like you're searching for someone. Not in a rushed way, but almost too calm, letting your head gradually shift from the other end to the other one, only once. This will allow the people in the room to see you and make you feel like you're fitting in, calmly searching for your friend even when there is no friend.

Once you're finished with the scan, focus your eyes on one person and give them a smile once you start walking into the crowd. This doesn't have to be a friend. If you can, do this to a stranger or, even better yet, to a hot man you're hoping to seduce. Doing the smile & walk move makes you seem approachable and makes others wonder what it would be like if that smile focused on them instead.

BECOME A HIGH VALUE WOMAN

A femme fatale is someone everyone wants to be with due to her appearance and behavior. Yet this behavior is not provocative or trashy. All femme fatales are high-value women. Femme fatales know their real value. They are desirable and have high standards towards themselves and others. They are highly valued and possess a deep sense of self-esteem and self-worth. These are all characteristics of a high-value woman.

The first step to becoming a high-value woman is to know your values and consider them in everything you do. Your actions should reflect your values, and you should never bargain for them.

High-value women are open-minded. Even though they have high standards and do not bargain regarding their values, high-value women know when to keep an open mind. These include social settings, first impressions, hobbies, new experiences, etc. Being open-minded makes a high-value woman more attractive and fun to be around.

A high-value woman does not take things personally and does not get easily offended. She knows who she is, as well as how the minds of other people work. She understands not to take someone's bad day or unintentional rude words personally and rarely lets the malicious intentions of others affect her. A high-value woman also does not hold grudges and understands the value of speaking up, talking things out, and making up. She does not quietly sulk when upset but speaks her mind and clears the air.

A high-value woman is a premium person who is not always available and, therefore, hard to get. She not only acts hard to get but has so many things going on in her life that she genuinely comes off that way. If you're lucky enough to spend some time with a high-value woman, you better make it worth her time.

A high-value woman always has a purpose. She does not simply just "hang around" to find out what she wants to do or stay in a job that she hates and complain about it to her friends. A high-value woman does not function from a lack mindset but instead always focuses on her goals.

Most importantly, a high-value woman is constantly improving herself personally, physically, and mentally. She has goals to become better in multiple aspects of her life and actively pursues them.

When a man crosses paths with a high-value woman, she does not drop everything and tend to his needs. She does not cancel her hobbies just to be able to schedule a date with him. She prioritizes her own life, and a man is only a bonus on the side if she has the time.

MASTERING THE ALLURE OF MYSTERY

Femme fatales are known to be mysterious, which is a big part of their allure.

It is an essential part of human nature that we will want to know more when we come across something that appears indistinct and vague. If you give someone a small detail but leave the rest out, the listener will usually want to know more. If movies, femme fatales generally appear out of nowhere, and we are left to wonder where they came from. We typically hear very little of their background stories, which makes us automatically imagine wild stories that might have been left untold.

Humans are naturally very curious and want to know more about things that are left untold or hidden. Someone who is mysterious engages and challenges our intellect as we try to use our imaginations to fill in the gaps.

Keep your agendas hidden

The first step to becoming mysterious is to keep your goals and aspirations hidden. This can be applied to any situation, both personal and professional.

When you're on a date, it's easy to state that you want to get married and have five kids. Keeping quiet about your intentions will keep the other party guessing what you're after.

If you're using your femme fatale seduction skills to entice someone to get closer to your goal, not talking about it will make it seem more genuine and not lead the other party to your intentions.

Finally, when you don't tell your goals, you improve your authority. This is because often when we start to pursue our goals, they take longer than expected or do not work the way we planned. If you had already told everyone what you planned to do, any changes in your plans would diminish your authority.

Keeping your goals and agendas hidden will make you seem mysterious and save you from losing your credibility.

Don't reveal too much

When you talk to people about yourself, try to tell them the bare minimum about yourself in a way that will make them want to ask more questions.

At its simplest, think about this example. If someone asks what your hobby is, try saying "water sports" instead of kayaking or "creative crafts" instead knitting.

This works because the person will automatically try to picture your hobby in their mind but will be unable to do so with the little information you've given.

They will feel inclined to ask more and, in their head, they are interested in you rather than you just rambling on about your hobby. Similarly, if someone asks about your weekend or any other experience, give them the larger picture rather than every little detail. This way, you'll trick their minds into getting interested using the basic human curiosity instinct.

This same rule should be applied to your social media behavior as well. Rather than posting exact images of yourself, post something that leaves space for imagination. Don't post a full-body image of yourself but perhaps a part of yourself, your scenery, or something you're doing. A big part of the mystery is having a mysterious social media presence as well.

Become unpredictable

A mysterious femme fatale is someone who cannot be put into a box. She is not someone who always goes for a run at 7 p.m. every evening, followed by a shower and then feeding her cat. She is not always available on Saturday nights at 5 p.m. and gives a radio silence at 11 p.m. Predictability is doing the same things or behaviors at the same exact times and ways so that others can predict what you do and when.

While it's good to have some routines, try to find ways to do your everyday things in a way. If you always reply to a man's text message within 5 minutes of receiving them, try occasionally waiting a bit longer.

Try to become unreliable in a way that doesn't necessarily harm your trustworthiness. By actually becoming busy in your life, you'll usually be able to appear more unpredictable in the eyes of others.

HOW TO MAKE A MAN OBSESSED WITH YOU

One of the key skills of a femme fatale is the ability to make any man obsessed with you. Despite the type of a man you're dealing with, the biological brain of men works relatively with the same mechanism. With certain intentional behaviors, you will be able to make anyone think about you obsessively, not being able to forget about you. Use these methods carefully, as intense obsession can become unhealthy and dangerous.

Trust in your power

Your internal mindset is the first prerequisite to getting a man obsessed with you. You must first trust in your power. If you find yourself doubting whether you're able to get people obsessed with you, that is your limiting beliefs talking, and you must first work to get rid of any negative thoughts. Getting someone obsessed with you starts with a mindset that your presence is a gift to anyone and that people are lucky to be around you. You must see your presence as something that brings value to others.

Make them feel special

Did you know that to make someone obsessed with you, it is more important to focus on how you make them feel instead of thinking about how they feel about you.

As a rule, humans like others who like them. The way to show someone that you like them is to make them feel special, not by words, but by a series of simple actions. Everyone wants to feel special, and we naturally gravitate toward those who make us feel that way.

The first step to making someone feel special is to listen to them. Genuinely hear what they say and actively listen. Active listening means having open and inviting body language. It also means asking follow-up questions about the topic your subject is talking about. Try to avoid asking close-ended questions that require a yes or no answer and try to ask open-ended questions instead. These questions will make your subject open about the topic further. Executed correctly, it will make them feel like you genuinely care about them.

The three-nod method is an excellent tool in your arsenal to become a great listener. When your subject has finished explaining something, hold eye contact and nod your head slowly three times while still looking into their eyes. This will make your subject feel like they want to keep talking more about the subject, further explaining themselves without you having to ask questions. When done moderately, this will add to the conversation, making it feel more natural and making them think they want to talk to you more.

Give the correct type of compliments

Giving compliments can be a great way to make someone feel special. For compliments to work as effectively as possible, you must carefully choose your words.

Simply telling a man "You're handsome" usually does not go a long way, especially if the man is very good-looking and hears it often. Think of how you can make your compliment more unusual so that your target will not be able to forget it. This way, he'll be unable to stop thinking about the compliment and you.

If you can, give compliments that make him feel slightly insecure. Instead of simply just telling someone they're handsome, you can say, "I forgot how handsome you are". This will make him wonder why you forgot and what you thought he was instead. It will also make him want to prove himself to you more than previously.

Become irreplaceable

To make a man obsessed with you find a way that you can become irreplaceable.

Most women do this the wrong way. They think that if they can get a man to rely on her cooking skills, he'll never leave or that she can become irreplaceable by frantically washing his laundry and carefully folding his underwear. This is not what becoming irreplaceable is.

Becoming irreplaceable is all about looking into the deep, dark, forgotten part of the man you're trying to seduce and seeing what his secret desires are. What does he want the most but can't have? What is the most significant contrast between what he wants to be and who he is? What does he long for the most? Find the missing peace and use the knowledge to your advantage.

Attention vs. withdrawal

Once you've made a man feel special, you've peaked their initial interest, but this does not yet make them obsessed with you.

At their core, men are hunters; without admitting to it or not, it is in their nature to chase women.

How often have you or your friend ended up in a situationship where the other person was always available, and the other person was never fully committing? The stories usually end with the always-available party getting hurt or heartbroken. This is because keeping the obsession and passion alive requires a balance of attention and withdrawal.

To get a man obsessed with you, you must first give attention to him and, the next minute, withdraw it. You must act in unpredictable ways. Make yourself so busy in your personal life that you sometimes forget to answer him or disappear for periods of time without any explanation.

If you're trying to make someone obsessed with you, they should not be your priority. Focus on yourself, your life, and other people around you. This will cause a man to wonder what you're doing, and they cannot help but find themselves obsessing over you.

If you're in a relationship and trying to make your boyfriend obsessed with you, all you must do is start prioritizing yourself a little more. Make some personal plans for yourself or with your friends, and do not ask his opinion. You do not need to start caring less; just prioritize yourself more. Your man will notice the difference. He'll notice the withdrawal, awakening his instinct to pursue you again.

HOW TO SEDUCE ANYONE

One of the most fascinating superpowers of a femme fatale is the ability to seduce anyone they choose as their target. While real life doesn't always work the way it does in the movies, learning these seduction techniques will take you ahead in the game. Using these, your target doesn't know what hit them.

1 – The first step of seduction is to initiate touch. Once you've chosen your target, your goal is to initiate small, subtle contact that will spark his interest and attraction. This doesn't mean kissing or getting in their way but the more subtle, the better.   You can think about accidentally brushing into them and apologizing for it. Or slightly brushing your leg over theirs while pretending to not notice you're doing it, or innocently brushing your fingers over their arm in a conversation.

2 – Seconds after you've initiated the first contact, withdraw physically while still holding eye contact. This will make them feel like you're not a threat and you're

getting away from them, but holding eye contact for longer than usual will raise their interest.

3 – Third way to seduce people is to play with your vulnerability. When you've done your shadow work, you can pinpoint exactly where your vulnerabilities lay so that you can use them in the process. Showing light on your vulnerabilities makes them feel you are genuine and will make them feel like they'll want to help you. This will make you more relatable and seem easier to approach.

4 – Make them feel like they're the only thing that matters. When you talk to them, only pay attention to them and no one else around them. Ask them questions that feel a bit extensive and that others might not consider asking. Validate their feelings and make them feel like the only one in the world for you, right until you withdraw the attention again. Be an active listener.

5 – Become the missing piece. By actively asking your target questions with the intention of finding out their weakness, you can find out what the person is missing the most in their life. This can be something that they

have missed in their childhood or feel that they are deprived of in the current moment.

We usually tend to want what we feel we are missing the most. This can be anything from affection, freedom, feeling appreciated, or being able to fully be ourselves.

By becoming the missing piece and acting as the part that this person is most deprived of, they will be undeniably seduced by you and unable to look away.

Attract, don't chase

Even though a femme fatale can seduce anyone, she doesn't do that by chasing men. In fact, femme fatales never chase men; they attract them.

Everything you do is carefully designed to attract your target to you, to make them come to you and think that they're trying to pursue you and not the other way around. This plays into their instincts as men and will make them do all the work for you.

Never desperately chase a man, no matter how much you desire their attention. As a rule, anyone you chase will only run away. By leaning back and letting the men do the work instead, you activate your dark feminine powers helping you realize who is actually putting in the effort and proving they are worth your time and energy.

BECOME AN ICONIC FEMME FATALE

Finally, what makes someone a femme fatale that is difficult to forget? The key on how to become an iconic femme fatale is all in personal branding.

The first step to becoming an iconic femme fatale is to choose the type of a dark feminine woman you want to become. This will become the foundation of what others see when they look at you and how they feel around you. Do you want to be known as a seductress? Do you want to be known as a daredevil that is full of adventure and magnificent stories? Do you want to become the epiphany of mysterious allure? Choosing your individual point of view will help you enforce your dark feminine energy to others.

Your signature perfume

Part of what makes a femme fatale unforgettable is her unique scent that invades your senses every time she crosses your mind.

As a femme fatale, you should choose a signature scent you will use most of the time. The scent you choose must be something that makes you feel sexy, mysterious, and seductive. It will be one of the most fundamental ways to channel your dark feminine energy and appear sensual in a way that becomes unexplainable to others.

Use your signature scent consistently, never going without it. Wear your signature scent even to bed.

If you're dating someone, slip on an extra spray of perfume just before romantic or sexual activities. This will imprint your scent into the other person, and they will be helpless in trying to get you out of their minds.

Typical dark femme fatale perfumes are the opposites of floral, airy, light feminine perfumes. They are heavy and rich and tend to have notes of leather, wood, or smoke. They are not necessarily sweet but have a muskier personality. Femme fatale fragrances are often associated with sophistication, elegance as well of mystery, and dark allure.

Finding your signature femme fatale scent can take a while. You should choose a perfume that describes your personality and that you're comfortable with.

Some excellent examples of femme fatale perfumes are:

- Santal Blush by Tom Ford
- Lady Vengeance by Juliette Has a Gun
- Hypnotic Poison by Dior
- L'Interdit by Givenchy
- Lost Cherry by Tom Ford
- Dark Purple by Montale

Consistency

The last tip for becoming an iconic femme fatale is to practice your newly learned skills on a regular basis. When you're doing something, ask yourself if it aligns with the ideal version of yourself. When wearing something, ask yourself if the ideal version of yourself would wear it.

Consistency is an integral part of personal branding, and when done correctly, people will start to associate you with the type of behavior you display on a regular basis. It will also imprint your new identity into your mind, helping you believe you are truly who you want to be. Being consistent with your femme fatale habits will make you recognizable among others, and they will start to associate you as a femme fatale with dark feminine qualities.

Whenever you feel like you need to be in alignment with what you want or who you want to become, refer back to the chapters in this book where you need help. Practice makes perfect; the more you practice, the more alluring femme fatale you become.

Finally, remember that femme fatales are never born, but they are created. By practicing the methods outlined in this book, you can become the powerful femme fatale beyond your dreams and transform your life beyond what you ever imagined possible.

Printed in Great Britain
by Amazon

35982861R00076